Roller Coaster!

Paul Mason

Raintree

Chicago, Illinois

© 2007 Raintree
Published by Raintree,
a division of Reed Elsevier Inc.
Chicago, Illinois

Customer Service   888–363–4266

Visit our website at www.heinemannraintree.com

Designed by Michelle Lisseter and Bridge
Creative Services
Picture Research by Hannah Taylor and Rebecca
Sodergren.
Printed and bound in China by WKT Company
Limited

11 10 09 08 07
10 9 8 7 6 5 4 3 2 1

**Library of Congress Cataloging-in-Publication
Data**
Mason, Paul, 1967-
  Roller coaster! / Paul Mason.
    p. cm.
  Includes bibliographical references and index.
  ISBN 1-4109-2587-0 (lib. bdg.) -- ISBN 1-4109-2616-
8 (pbk.)
  1. Force and energy--Juvenile literature. 2. Motion--
Juvenile literature. 3. Roller coasters--Juvenile
literature. I. Title.
  QC73.4.M3875 2006
  531'.11--dc22

                                        2006008792

13 digit ISBNs
978-1-4109-2587-9 (hardcover)
978-1-4109-2616-6 (paperback)

Acknowledgments
The author and publisher are grateful to the
following for permission to reproduce copyright
material: Alamy Images p. **15** inset (David Sanger
Photography), **22–23** (David Wall); Corbis p. **8**
(Jeffry W. Myers), **14–15** (Richard Cummins), **16–17**
(Tony Arruza); Getty Images/Photonica p. **25** inset;
Getty Images/Stone pp. **20–21**; Getty Images/
Taxi pp. **26–27**; Lonely Planet Images pp. **6–7**
(Richard Cummins); masterfile pp. **4–5** (Roy Ooms);
masterfile/Rommel pp.**18–19**, **24–25**; Photolibrary.
com p. **13**; Photolibrary.com/Index Stock Imagery
pp. **10–11**; Reuters p. **9** (Haruyoshi Yamaguchi).

Cover photograph of double loop roller coaster
reproduced with permission of Corbis (Lester
Lefkowitz).

Illustrations by Bridge Creative Services.

The publishers would like to thank Nancy Harris and
Harold Pratt for their assistance in the preparation of
this book.

Contents

Some words are printed in bold, **like this**. You can find out what they mean on page 30. You can also look in the box at the bottom of the page where they first appear.

Design Your Own Roller Coaster!

There are roller coasters all around the world. Roller coaster rides are very popular and thrilling. People travel a long way to enjoy these rides.

Roller coasters can travel at over 100 miles (160 kilometers) per hour. But they do not have engines! Their **speed** comes from whizzing down their first hill. This is called the **lift hill**.

That's amazing!

The world's fastest roller coaster opened in 2005. It is in Jackson, New Jersey. It is called Kingda Ka. It is 456 feet (139 meters) high and it travels at 128 miles (206 kilometers) per hour!

Roller coasters are ▶ terrifying, but fun!

lift hill first hill on a roller coaster ride
speed distance traveled in a set period of time
vertical straight up and down

Imagine that you could build your own roller coaster. How would you design it? Would there be loops and twists? Would there be **vertical** (straight up and down) drops? Read on to find out the secrets of roller coaster design!

▼ Imagine sitting down to design your own roller coaster. What would it look like?

656 feet (200 meters)

164 feet (50 meters)

328 feet (100 meters)

Newton's First Law of Motion

Before you design your roller coaster, there is one bit of science you need to learn. It is Newton's First Law of Motion. A **force** is a push or a pull. The First Law says that objects only start moving if a force acts on them. The First Law also says a force can make a moving object speed up. It can make it slow down or change **direction**.

What does this mean for you, as a roller coaster designer? It means you will need a force. The more forces you use, the more fun your ride will be!

No forces are acting on the roller coaster to make it change direction.

direction	course along which something moves
force	push or pull

▼ A force is needed to make the roller coaster move. In this book, forces are shown by green arrows.

The passengers are not that thrilled . . . yet!

7

That's amazing!

The world's longest roller coaster is the Steel Dragon in Japan. The ride is 1.5 miles (2.5 kilometers) long!

What Goes Up . . .

At the start of the ride you are designing, the train of cars sits still. No **force** is acting on it. It does not move.

Next, the train slowly starts to move uphill. A force is acting on it. The train is pulled up the tracks by a motor. It goes uphill against the force of **gravity**. Gravity is a force that pulls all things down toward the center of Earth.

The force of the motor is greater than ▼ the force of gravity. The roller coaster is pulled up to the top of the first hill. The first hill is called the lift hill.

A motor pulls the cars uphill.

gravity   force that pulls objects toward the center of Earth

▼ *Now, the force of gravity is greater. The roller coaster is pulled down.*

The force of gravity pulls the cars down.

That's scary!

*The steepest downslopes on roller coasters are almost **vertical** (straight down)!*

...must come down!

Now, half the train is over the top of the **lift hill**. Things start to happen a lot quicker. Gravity pulls the train downhill. It goes faster and faster.

Gravity is the main force you will use in your roller coaster design. It slows your train down going uphill. It speeds it up going downhill.

On Track for Thrills

Your train reaches the bottom of the slope. It is going fast in a straight line. What can stop it from traveling in a straight line? The answer is the tracks. The train goes where the tracks go. If the tracks curl around, the train goes around. The tracks provide the **force** (push or pull) that changes the **direction** of the train.

The **speed** and direction together are called **velocity**. To change the velocity, you must change the speed or the direction. The more this happens, the better the ride!

Did you know?

The world's first roller coaster with wheels opened in 1817. It was in Paris, France.

velocity   speed in a particular direction

Newton's First Law of Motion makes cars want to go in a straight line.

roller coaster wheels

The force of the tracks pushes back against the wheels.

11

Your heart in your mouth!

Your passengers whoosh up and down. This makes them feel funny. Over the top of each hill, it feels as though their insides are rising up inside them! Why does this happen?

- A **force** (push or pull) changes the **direction** of the cars. The track provides the force. It pulls the cars downward. The cars start moving down.

- **Gravity** also pulls the cars downward. The cars go faster.

- The riders' bodies are held inside the cars. They change direction, too.

- The insides of the passengers, just for a moment, obey Newton's First Law of Motion. They continue moving in a straight line—upward!

- The passengers hit the bottom of the slope. The opposite happens. Now, it feels as though their insides are being pulled down inside them!

Top hat!

Stealth is the fastest roller coaster in Europe. It is in the United Kingdom. People call it a top hat. It takes passengers straight up, then straight down—all in fifteen seconds!

The force of gravity pulls the cars down to the bottom of the slope.

The passengers' insides obey Newton's Law. They travel straight down—but just for a moment!

Twists and turns

There are many ways to make your roller coaster change **direction**. It does not only have to go up and down. You can also design twists and turns. These will make it go from side to side, too!

Roller coaster designers often make their trains change direction in more than one way at the same time. Here are some examples:

- A sudden turn with a downward drop will make your passengers feel as if they are about to fly off into space.

- A sudden turn at the bottom of a slope will make them feel as if the train is going to topple over sideways.

There are a lot of other combinations! Are you starting to get some ideas for how to make your roller coaster the best ever?

Hold tight!

The first lap bar was used in 1907. It held passengers safely inside a roller coaster car.

▼ The passengers' bodies try to go in a straight line. They are carried around the corner by the train.

lap bar

Passengers' bodies try to go straight.

Tracks curve to the left.

15

Some roller coasters ▶ even hang from the tracks!

Losing Speed

Every time your train goes uphill, it slows down. It loses **speed**. **Gravity** begins to act on the train. Gravity pulls it down and backward. This slows it down.

The train then gets most of its speed back. It does this by going down the other side of the hill. But some of the speed has been lost forever.

Every time a roller ▶ *coaster goes uphill, it loses some of its speed.*

gravity pulls downward

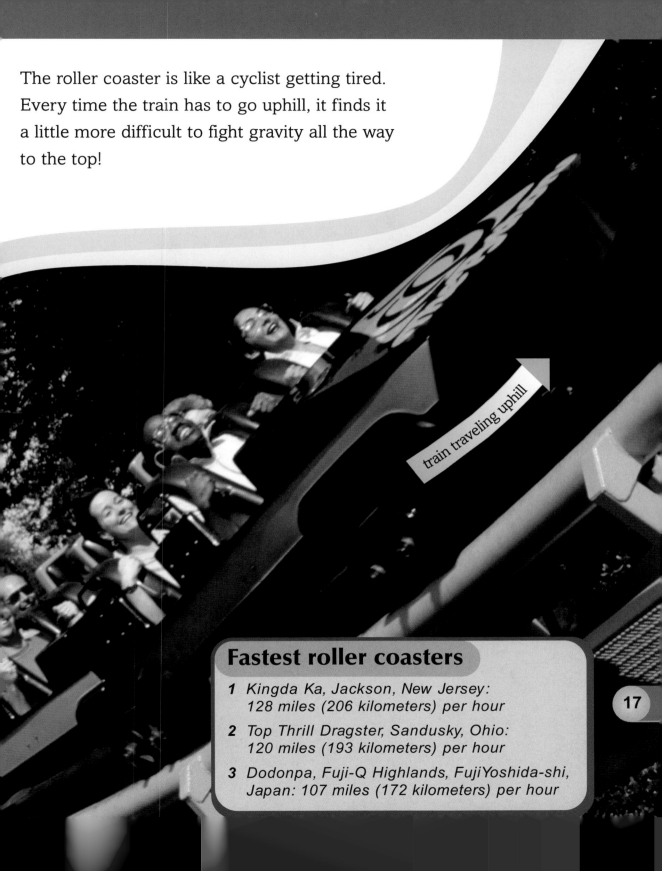

The roller coaster is like a cyclist getting tired. Every time the train has to go uphill, it finds it a little more difficult to fight gravity all the way to the top!

train traveling uphill

Fastest roller coasters

1 *Kingda Ka, Jackson, New Jersey: 128 miles (206 kilometers) per hour*

2 *Top Thrill Dragster, Sandusky, Ohio: 120 miles (193 kilometers) per hour*

3 *Dodonpa, Fuji-Q Highlands, FujiYoshida-shi, Japan: 107 miles (172 kilometers) per hour*

Friction

Your roller coaster train loses **speed** as it goes uphill. But it also loses speed when it goes around bends. Why does this happen?

The reason is a **force** called **friction**. Friction affects objects that rub against each other. It slows them down. For example, when you pull on a bicycle's brakes, the brakes touch the wheel. This creates friction. Friction is what slows down the bicycle.

Your roller coaster slows down in a similar way. Its wheels rub against the tracks, causing friction. This slows down the roller coaster.

Too many corners will slow down your roller coaster!

19

Air resistance

Air resistance will also slow down your roller coaster. Air resistance is a kind of **friction**. The roller coaster and its passengers push against the air. The air slows them down.

Because the train loses **speed** during the ride, none of the hills on your roller coaster can be higher than the **lift hill**. Otherwise, the train will not make it to the top. Your passengers will find themselves sliding backward!

That's amazing!

The first roller coaster to make a loop was in the Frascati Garden in Paris, France. The year was 1846!

air resistance force of air pushing against an object

These passengers look like they are making funny faces! In fact, the passing air is forcing their skin into strange shapes.

21

Slower and Lower

Remember Newton's First Law of Motion? Your moving object (the roller coaster train) is slowing down. All the **forces** (push and pulls) have slowed down the train. It may only have enough **speed** left for one more big change of **direction**! What will you decide to do? You could:

- Throw in a lot of little changes of direction. They would confuse and amaze your passengers. The small forces used will not slow down the train too much. You will be able to stretch the ride out for longer.

- Use all your speed in one try! You could put a steep hill and a tight turn in together. You could even add several tight turns. This is called a corkscrew! That would be a dramatic finish.

That's confusing!

To make things even scarier, some roller coasters run backward!

23

▲ *Will you finish off the ride with a thrilling corkscrew section?*

The Best Seat on the Train

As a roller coaster designer, you will need to try out a lot of different rides. This will help you decide which ones are most exciting. But where is the best place to sit?

At the front

The front is where you get the best view. All the twists, turns, rises, and falls come as a surprise.

Looking down ▼ from the front is scary . . .

That's wild!

Roller coasters with just one car are called "wild mouse" rides.

At the back

Not all the cars in the train are pulled downward by **gravity** alone. Some are also pulled by the cars in front of them. As the first car goes over the hill, it starts to be pulled downward by gravity. Then, the first car pulls on the cars behind. The ride is a little bit more extreme at the back!

. . . but the ride at the back ▼ might be more thrilling!

Back Where It All Began

Have you done your design job well? The train of cars will hardly be moving when it rolls back to the start. All the **speed** has been used up. The **friction** of the twists, turns, ups, and downs has slowed down the roller coaster. The train rolls back to the start. Its last drop of speed has been used up.

That's thrilling!

Some roller coasters have seats that spin around. The first one was opened in 2002. It was in Valencia, California.

▼ *Will your passengers leave your ride wanting more? Or will they be so scared they go straight home?*

Your passengers are living examples of Newton's First Law of Motion. **Forces** have made them turn left and right. Forces have made them speed up and slow down. Forces have pushed and pulled them around the track.

Finally, at the end, they might be glad the ride has stopped!

27

Rolling Around the World

These are some of the world's most famous roller coasters and parks. People travel thousands of miles to ride them! Could you design a ride as thrilling as these?

Name: Kingda Ka
Location: Jackson, N.J.
Opened: 2005
The tallest, fastest roller coaster in the world!

Name: Cedar Point
Location: Sandusky, Ohio
Opened: 1870
This park has more record-breaking roller coasters than any other park in the world.

Name: Six Flags Magic Mountain
Location: Valencia, California
Opened: 1971
A roller coaster park. Sixteen are in one place.

Name: SheiKra
Location: Tampa Bay, Florida
Opened: 2005
The tallest dive of any roller coaster: 200 feet (61 meters) straight down!

Name: Oblivion
Location: Staffordshire, UK
Opened: 1998
The first roller coaster ever to have a **vertical** drop.

Name: Colossus
Location: Surrey, UK
Opened: 2002
The first roller coaster to turn its passengers upside down ten times!

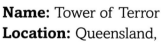

Name: Dragon Khan
Location: Salou, Spain
Opened: 1995
A ride based on the legend of a Chinese dragon that became angry whenever a human climbed on its back!

Name: Fuji-Q Highlands
Location: Yamanashi, Japan
Opened: 1961
Fujiyama and Dodonpa are rides in this park. They are both among the top-ten fastest roller coasters.

Name: Tower of Terror
Location: Queensland, Australia
Opened: 1997
When it was built, this was the fastest roller coaster in the world, at 100 miles (160 kilometers) per hour.

Glossary

air resistance force of air pushing against an object. You can feel air resistance blowing your hair back when you ride your bike.

direction course along which something moves. For example, forward, backward, up, down, right, or left.

force push or pull. For example, you use a force when you push on the pedals of a bike to ride it along. You pull on a door handle to make a door open.

friction force that can slow down moving objects. Friction happens when two surfaces rub against each other.

gravity force that pulls objects toward the center of Earth. The force of gravity is what keeps you on the ground.

lift hill first hill on a roller coaster ride. The higher the lift hill, the faster a roller coaster can travel.

speed distance traveled in a set period of time. The fastest roller coasters can travel at well over 100 miles (160 kilometers) per hour!

velocity speed in a particular direction. Changes in velocity make roller coasters fun!

vertical straight up and down. Several roller coasters have vertical drops.

Roller-glossary

Here are some technical roller coaster terms you might find useful:

mine train roller coaster designed to give the experience of riding a runaway mine train. They usually follow the shape of the land closely. They make small but quick drops and turns.

shuttle roller coaster that travels to the end of its track and returns in the opposite direction. A shuttle roller coaster's track has a beginning and end. A traditional roller coaster begins and ends at the same place.

sit-down traditional roller coaster, which is ridden sitting down

stand-up roller coaster ridden while standing up instead of sitting down

suspended roller coaster with trains that travel beneath the track. They hang from a swinging arm and turn from side to side. It makes the turns much more exciting.

twin roller coaster with two tracks. The tracks often follow a similar course. It feels as if the trains are racing each other.

wild mouse ride using single-car trains on a track with very tight turns

Want to Know More?

Books

- Baine, Celeste. *The Fantastical Engineer: A Thrillseeker's Guide to Careers in Theme Park Engineering.* Calhoun, La.: Bonamy, 2000.
  This is a great book for anyone who wants to design roller coasters or other amusement-park attractions.
- Burgan, Michael. *The World's Wildest Roller Coasters.* Mankato, Minn.: Capstone, 2001.
  This describes some of the world's great roller coaster rides and some different types of roller coaster. It also explains how they work.

Websites

- http://www.aceonline.org
  Visit the website of the American Coaster Enthusiasts Club. Find out about roller coasters in North America.
- http://www.learner.org/exhibits/parkphysics/coaster
  Visit this site to get help as you attempt to design the world's best roller coaster. At the end of the process, your roller coaster gets a "safety rating" and a "fun rating," plus a review of the features included in your design.

Find out how gravity works in skateboarding and other extreme sports in *The Extreme Zone*.

It is possible to escape gravity. Find out how in *10 Experiments Your Teacher Never Told You About*.

Index